DRAGONMAZIA

ROLF HEIMANN

www.littleharebooks.com

Little Hare Books
8/21 Mary Street, Surry Hills
NSW 2010 AUSTRALIA

www.littleharebooks.com

First published in 2008

National Library of Australia

Cataloguing-in-Publication entry

Heimann, Rolf, 1940-

Dragonmazia / author, Rolf Heimann.

Surry Hills, N.S.W. : Little Hare Books, 2008.

978 1 921 272 49 3 (pbk.)

Puzzles--Juvenile literature.
Dragons--Juvenile literature.

793.73

Designed by Bernadette Gethings
Produced in Singapore by Pica Digital
Printed in China through Phoenix Offset

5 4 3 2 1

1. Twin Dragons

These two dragons look the same but there are ten differences. Can you spot them?

2. Mini Maze

From one side of the egg to the other—can you make it through?

3. Speedy Dragons

The blue dragon can fly fifty kilometres in an hour. The green dragon can fly twenty kilometres in half an hour. The red dragon can fly twice as fast as the green dragon. Which dragon is the fastest?

4. Dragon Breath

Can you make your way through this maze of flames? Follow the arrows to help find your way. Don't get lost! It's hot in there!

5. Dragon Eggs

There is a path through this maze that connects all four dragon nests. Can you find your way through? Start at nest one.

6. A Dragon Gatekeeper!

This dragon gatekeeper will only let dragons into the castle if they can make it through the maze first. Can you help the little dragon through?

7. Dragon Time

The dragon gatekeeper also likes clocks—but he always forgets to set them correctly. One always shows the right time. One is five minutes fast. One is ten minutes slow. And one does not work at all. What is the correct time?

8. The Dragon's Tail

To open the gate does the dragon have to lower his tail or lift it?

9. Dragon Wall

Fourteen tiles have fallen off this ancient Chinese wall. Are you able to put each one back where it belongs?

10. Something Strange

There is something different about this dragon. Can you see what it is?

11. Hidden Dragon, Sleeping Dragon

You can't fly a kite without a string. But how will you get from the kite to the reel of string? It might be safer to go through the maze and past the sleeping dragon than through the woods!

There are two ways through this maze—one that goes over the bridge and past the dragon's nose and a second way that avoids bridge altogether. Can you find them both?

12. Flying Flags

Something spoils the symmetry in this display of flags. Can you spot it?

13. Starry Maze

You enter this maze at the top. But don't expect to go downhill all the way!

14. Dragon Hide-and-See

These little dragons like to hide, their tails give them away! How r little dragons can YOU find?

5. The Dragon Twist

nese twisted dragons are trying
bite each other's tails. But
nose tails are they really
ting? Take a look, you will be
rprised!

16. Spot-the-difference!

They might be brothers, but there are five differences between them. Can you spot them?

17. Mazes Apart

The two mini-mazes in the corners of this page may look the same, but they're not. Work your way through both mazes just to make sure!

18. Help Build a Dragon Nest

This dragon is collecting reeds for her nest. But it has to be the rare 'Silvery Dragon Reed'. She has found one, but needs five more. Can you help her find them?

19. Who's Afraid of Dragons?

The green dragonflies, believe it or not, are afraid of dragons. That is why they hide themselves amongst the 'Silvery Dragon Reed' as soon as a dragon appears. How many can you find?
Don't confuse them with the blue-tailed caterpillar!

TO: Sir Short-Tail-
Yellow-Spots-Three-Horn
The Dungeon of Slime
1 Princess Street
Ever After

20. Detective Work

Can you deliver this letter to the right dragon?

21. Dragon of Wales

This is the famous dragon flag of Wales. On the right is a copy of it. Look closely: there are five mistakes in the copy and you need to find them!

22. Hatched Dragon

The eggs in these three nests look very similar, but they are actually from different species of dragon. Which of the three species does this newborn dragon come from? A, B or C.

23. Red Dragon to Green Dragon

Find a way through the maze from the red dragon to the green dragon.

24. Enter the Dragon's Mouth!

Climb into the dragon's mouth (if you dare!) and quickly find your way out! Only one of the twelve exits works!

25. Five Little Dragons

Which of the five dragons on the black panel belongs in the black space on the left?

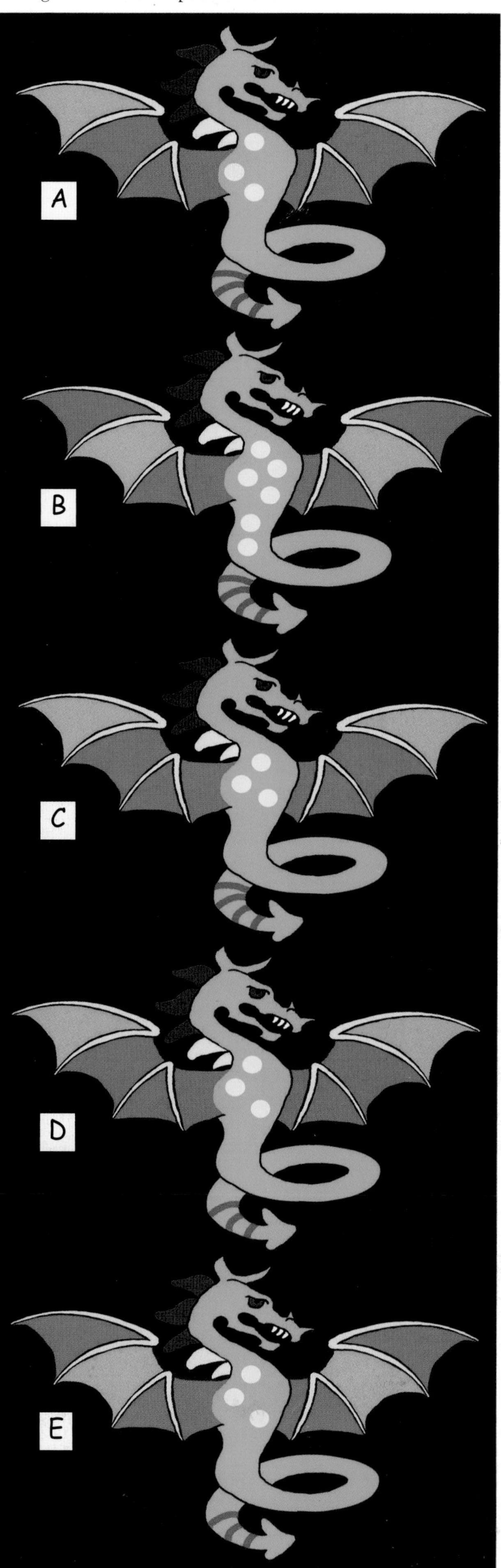

26. An Amaze-ing Tattoo!

Here's a dragon who truly loves mazes! He's even had one tattooed to
chest! Can you find your way from the top to the bottom of his tattoo

27. Maze Collector

He's making himself a cup of tea to calm his nerves. He ha
discovered that one of the mazes in his collection is imposs
to go through. Which one is it?

28. Tea?

This dragon lov
tea almost as m
his mazes. He h
different flavou
drink eac
Can you
which da

MAZE
MONDA
SUNDAY
TUESDAY
WEDNESDAY
THURSDAY
FRIDAY
SATURDAY

29. Optic Dragons

These two dragons are trying to see each other but can't. Can you help them through the maze?

30. Individuals

Each of these five dragons has one thing that makes it different from all the others. Can you name the different feature of each dragon

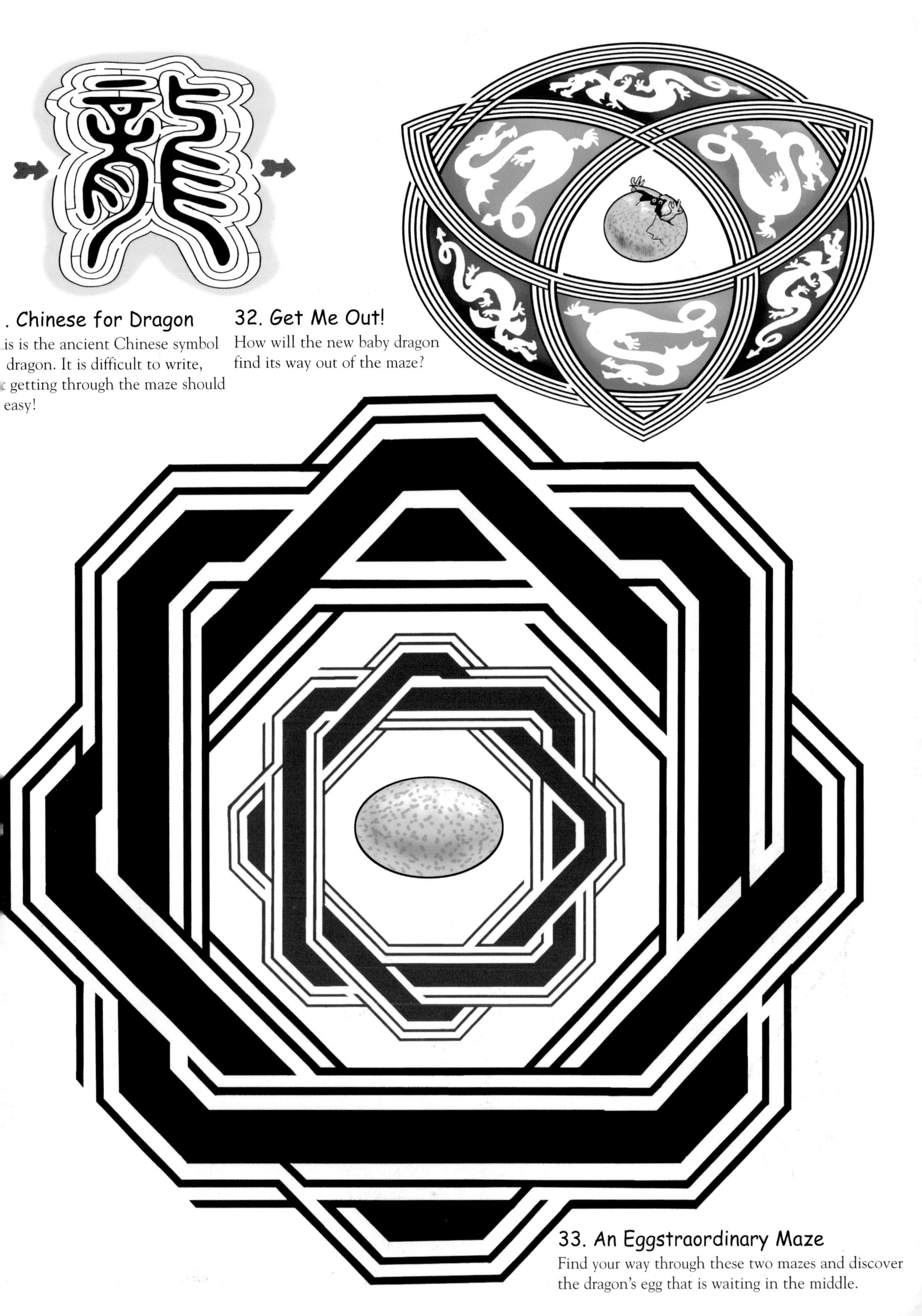

. Chinese for Dragon

is is the ancient Chinese symbol dragon. It is difficult to write, getting through the maze should easy!

32. Get Me Out!

How will the new baby dragon find its way out of the maze?

33. An Eggstraordinary Maze

Find your way through these two mazes and discover the dragon's egg that is waiting in the middle.

34. The Dragon's Lair

The sacred lake seems to give a perfect mirror image. But look closely. Fourteen things are wrongly reflected.

35. Dragonese

Dragons have their very own language! Can you read the signs?

Here are some clues to help you:

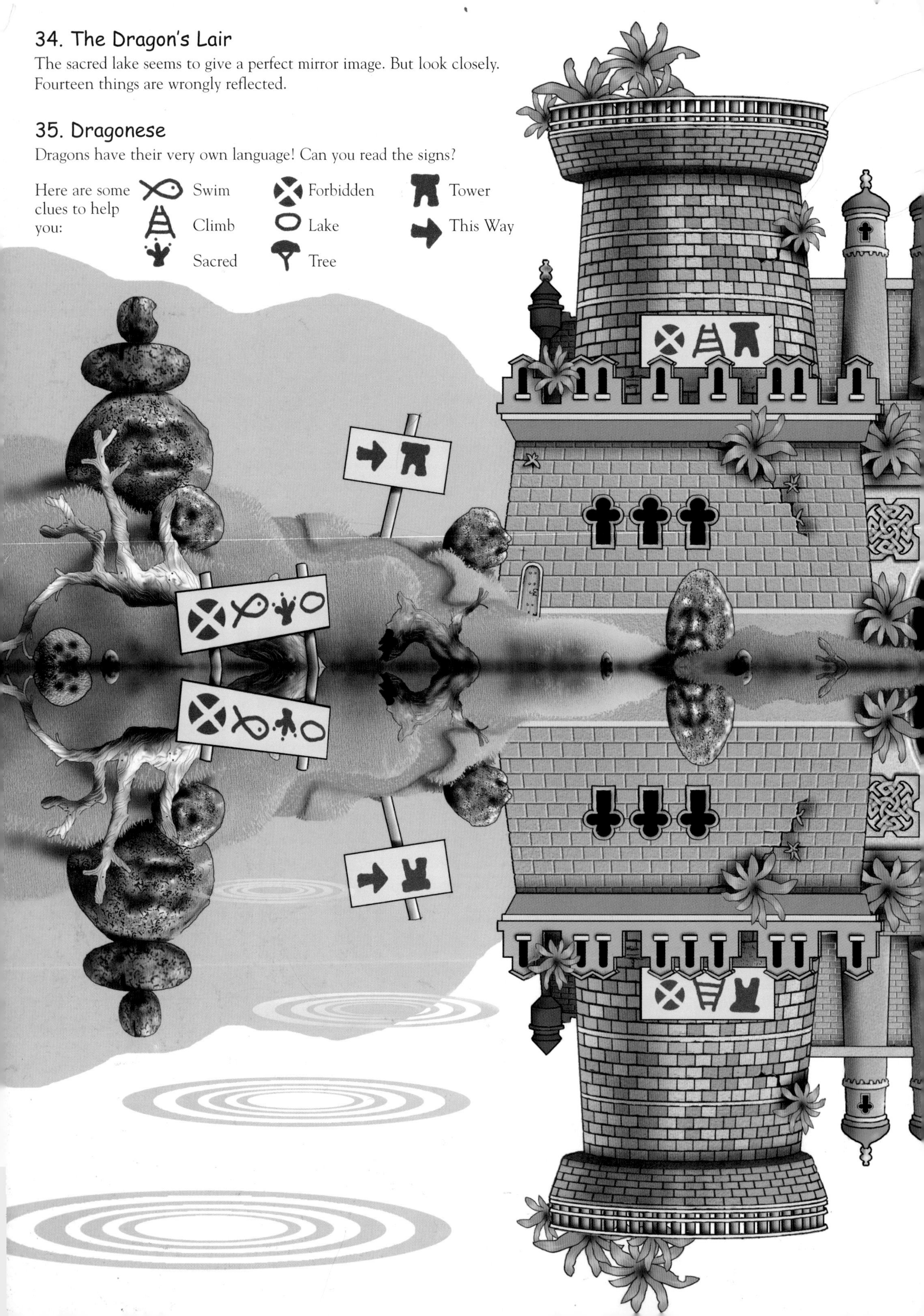

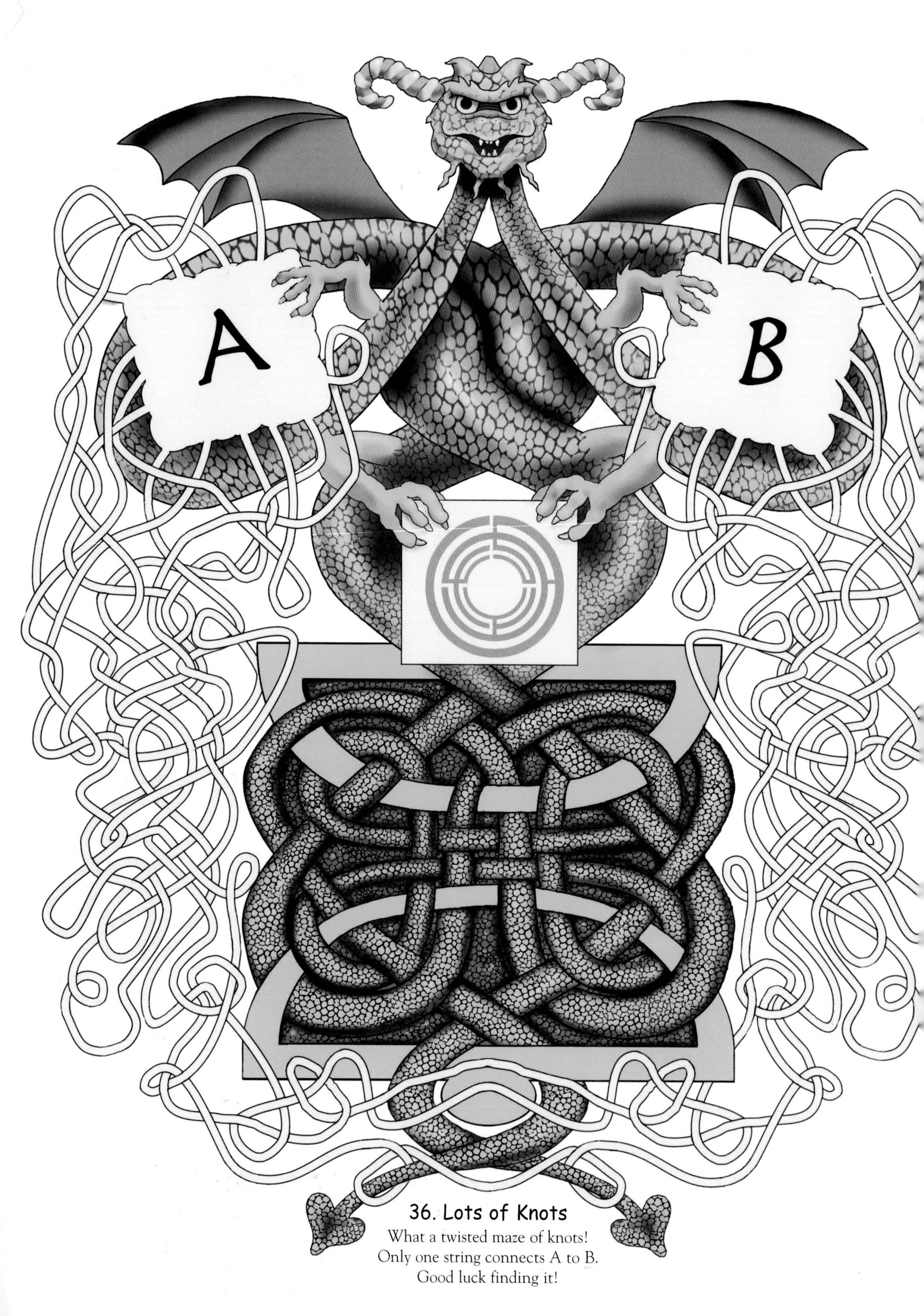

36. Lots of Knots

What a twisted maze of knots!
Only one string connects A to B.
Good luck finding it!

37. Mama Dragon and Baby Dragon

Can you help this dragon mother and her child? The only path is through this very tricky maze!

38. The Changing of the Flags

The green dragon standing at the flag pole needs to take one of the flags to the empty pole on the opposite side of the maze. Can you help him get there by the blue path?

39. The Hardest Maze of All!

First you need to find the stripy snake. He wants to help himself to all of the dragon eggs but he can't cross over the blue or red lines. How many eggs are safe?

Solutions

1. Twin Dragons:
The differences have been circled.

2. Mini Maze:
Follow the red line through the maze.

3. Speedy Dragons:
The red dragon.

4. Dragon Breath:
Follow the black line through the maze.

5. Dragon Eggs:
Follow the red line through the maze.

6. A Dragon Gatekeeper!:
Follow the red line through the maze.

7. Dragon Time: The correct time is circled.

8. The Dragon's Tail: The dragon has to lower his tail.

9. Dragon Wall: The numbers match up where the correct tiles belong.

10. Something Strange: He has five legs!

11. Hidden Dragon, Sleeping Dragon: Follow the red lines through the maze to discover the two paths.

12. Flying Flags: The first and last flags are not exactly the same. One has a blue diamond shape on one side, and the other is coloured red.

13. Starry Maze:
Follow the red line through the maze.

14. Dragon Hide-and-Seek:
There are seven dragons.
Did you remember to count the dragon sitting on the rock?

15. The Dragon Twist:
This puzzle is an optical illusion! The two tails are connected to each other, and the two bodies are connected to each other. Look again.

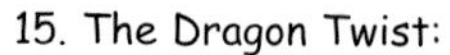

16. Spot-the-difference!:
The differences have been circled. There are two differences on the tails, but the tails are not connected to the brothers!

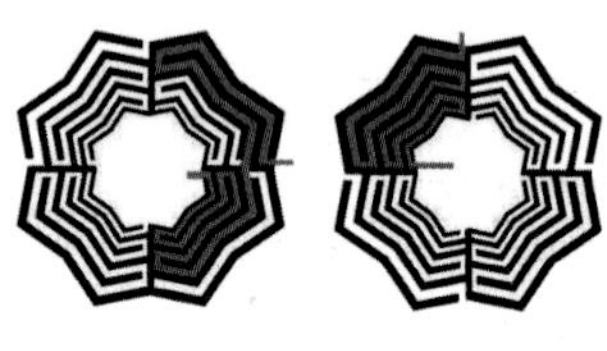

17. Mazes Apart: These two mazes have very different paths. Follow the red line in each puzzle.

. Help Build a Dragon Nest: There are arrows next to the
e 'Silvery Dragon Reeds'.

. Who's Afraid of Dragons?:
nere are seven
agonflies. They
ve been circled.

). Detective Work: The letter should be delivered to:

1. Dragon of Wales:
he mistakes have been circled.

2. Hatched Dragon: B

3. Red Dragon to Green Dragon:
ollow the red line through the maze.

4. Enter the Dragon's Mouth!:
ollow the blue line through the maze.

5. Five Little Dragons: D

6. An Amaze-ing Tattoo:
ollow the red line through the maze.

7. Maze Collector: The arrow points
the impossible maze.

28. Tea?: Tuesday

29. Optic Dragons: Follow the
ed line through the maze.

30. Individuals: The first dragon
has spots, the second has a tongue,
he third has no wings, the fourth has
o legs and the fifth has three tails!

31. Chinese for Dragon: Follow the red line through the maze.

32. Get Me Out!: Follow the red
line through the maze.

33. An Eggstraordinary
Maze:
The red line shows the
path through the outer maze
and the black line through
the inner maze.

34. The Dragon's Lair:
The fourteen changes have
been circled.

35. Dragonese: 1. No swimming in the sacred lake. 2. This way to the tower.
3. No climbing the tower. 4. No climbing the sacred tree.

36. Lots of Knots: The red string is the correct path.

37. Mama Dragon and Baby Dragon: Follow the red line through the maze.

38. The Changing of the Flags: Follow the black path.

39. The Hardest Maze of All!: Six eggs. The light blue area indicates the
space that can be reached by the snake.

Rolf Heimann was born in Dresden, Germany in 1940. In 1945, he witnessed the total destruction of his home city—which made him a lifelong opponent of war.

At age 18 he migrated to Australia. Over the next few years he worked his way around the country doing all kinds of jobs, including fruit-picking, labouring at railways and working in factories. Every spare hour was spent writing and sketching. Eventually, he settled in Melbourne, where he worked for printers and publishers before finally running his own art studio.

In 1974, Rolf sailed his own boat around the Pacific (and met his future wife, Lila, in Samoa), returning to Australia after two years to concentrate on painting, writing, cartooning and illustrating. He has now published over fifty books, including puzzle and maze books, junior novels and picture books. His books have travelled to dozens of countries and have sold millions of copies around the world.

Also by Rolf Heimann from Little Hare Books:

DINOMAZIA

ROLF'S CORNY COPIA

PUZZLEMAZIA

CRAZY COSMOS

BRAIN BUSTING BONANZA

ASTROMAZE

ZOODIAC

ROLF'S FLUMMOXING FLABBERGASTERS

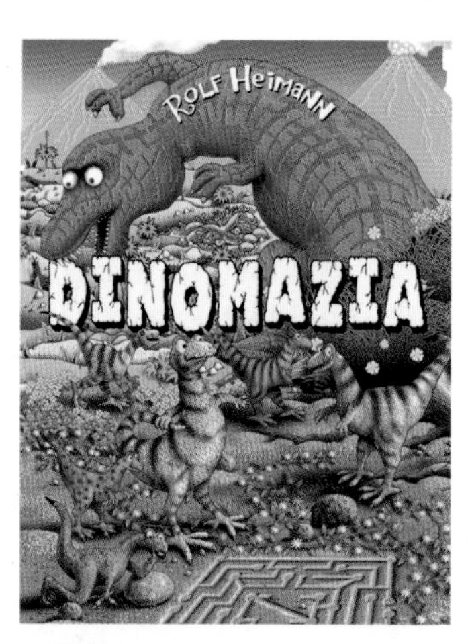

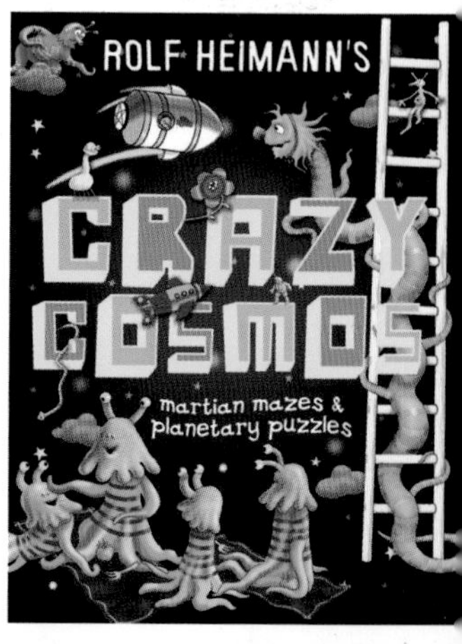